Collins

easy learning

Phonics
bumper book

Ages
3–5

boat

Carol Medcalf

How to use this book

- Find a quiet, comfortable place to work, away from distractions.

- This book has been written in a logical order, so start at the first page and work your way through.

- Help with reading the instructions where necessary and ensure that your child understands what to do.

- This book is a gentle introduction to the sounds of the English language. Working through the book, your child will start to realise that words are made up of small separate sounds, called phonemes, e.g. **cat** is made up of three phonemes: **c-a-t**. Encourage your child to sound out each phoneme before they attempt to read the whole word, e.g. say 'kuh-a-tuh' and then read 'cat'. Some phonemes are represented by two or three letters, such as **sh** and **igh**. Your child should sound out the single **sh** or **igh** sound and not the individual letter sounds. Where this occurs the letters are underlined to show that they make one sound.

- Children learn and develop at their own rate. If an activity is too difficult for your child then do more of our suggested practical activities (see Parent's tips) and return to the page when you know that they're likely to achieve it.

- Always end each activity before your child gets tired so that they will be eager to return next time.

- Help and encourage your child to check their own answers as they complete each activity.

- Let your child return to their favourite pages once they have been completed. Talk about the activities they enjoyed and what they have learned.

Special features of this book:

- **Yellow box:** situated at the top of each page, this gives an example word containing the sound so that you can ensure your child is learning the correct sound.

- **Parent's tip:** situated on every left-hand page, this suggests further activities and encourages discussion about what your child has learned.

- **Progress panel:** situated at the bottom of every right-hand page, the number of stars shows your child how far they have progressed through the book. Once they have completed each double page, ask them to colour in the blank star.

- **Certificate:** the certificate on the last page should be used to reward your child for their effort and achievement. Remember to give your child plenty of praise and encouragement, regardless of how they do.

Useful definitions

- **Phoneme** – a unit of sound.
- **Grapheme** – a letter or number of letters that represent a unit of sound (a phoneme).
- **Digraph** – a sound represented by two letters, e.g. **sh** and **th**.
- **Trigraph** – a sound represented by three letters, e.g. **igh**.
- **Sound button** – dots and underscores used to show the separate graphemes that make up a word.
- **Sound family** – two or more graphemes that make the same sound, e.g. **c**, **k** and **ck**.

Published by Collins
An imprint of HarperCollins*Publishers* Ltd
The News Building
1 London Bridge Street
London
SE1 9GF

Browse the complete Collins catalogue
at www.collins.co.uk

© HarperCollins*Publishers* Ltd 2018

10 9 8 7

ISBN 9780008275433

The author asserts the moral right to be identified as the author of this work.

All rights reserved. No part of this publication may be reproduced, stored in a retrieval system, or transmitted, in any form or by any means, electronic, mechanical, photocopying, recording or otherwise, without the prior permission of Collins.

British Library Cataloguing in Publication Data

A Catalogue record for this publication is available from the British Library

All images and illustrations are
© Shutterstock.com and
© HarperCollins*Publishers*

Author: Carol Medcalf
Commissioning Editor: Michelle l'Anson
Project Manager: Rebecca Skinner
Cover Design: Sarah Duxbury
Text Design and Layout: QBS Learning
Illustration: Jenny Tulip
Production: Natalia Rebow
Printed in Great Britain by Bell and Bain Ltd.

Contents

Phonic sound s

s, as in **sun**.

● Circle all the things that start with the **s** sound.

It is most important when teaching phonics to sound the letter out correctly. If your child hears and learns the wrong sound, it will make learning to read much harder. Listen to sounds on the internet before saying them if you are not sure of the correct sound.

Phonic sound a

a, as in **apple**.

● Draw a line from the fishing rod to each fish that has a picture starting with the **a** sound.

Well done! Now colour the star.

Phonic sound t

t, as in **tap**.

● Colour each section that has a picture starting with the **t** sound.

● Colour these pictures that start with the **t** sound.

To help with speech sounds you can do some fun facial exercises, such as making funny faces: screw your face up, puff it out, make it thin, wiggle your tongue around.

Phonic sound p

p, as in **pen**.

● Find the **p**irate treasure by joining all the words that start with the **p** sound.

Phonic sound i

i, as in **ink**.

● Draw a line to send an **i**nvitation to each **i**gloo.

● Circle the **i** sound in each word.

p**i**nk　　　t**i**n　　　b**i**n　　　**i**nk

Blowing is a good exercise for facial muscles. You can blow bubbles, use drinking straws to blow a splodge of paint around paper to make a picture, or roll a ball along the floor by blowing it – have a race and see who wins!

Phonic sound n

n, as in **nose**.

● Colour all the pictures that start with the **n** sound.

Phonic sound m

m, as in **map**.

● Circle and say the **m** sound in each word.

melon   milk   meerkat

money   monkey

● Say the sound as you write the letter.

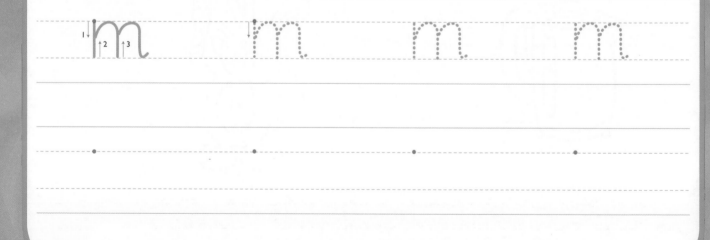

Listening games are really important. Your child needs to be able to listen to hear the phonetic sounds in words. To develop listening, go on a sound walk and talk about what you can hear.

Phonic sound d

d, as in **dog**.

● Name the animals.
  Tick (✓) the animal that will reach the **d**oughnut first.

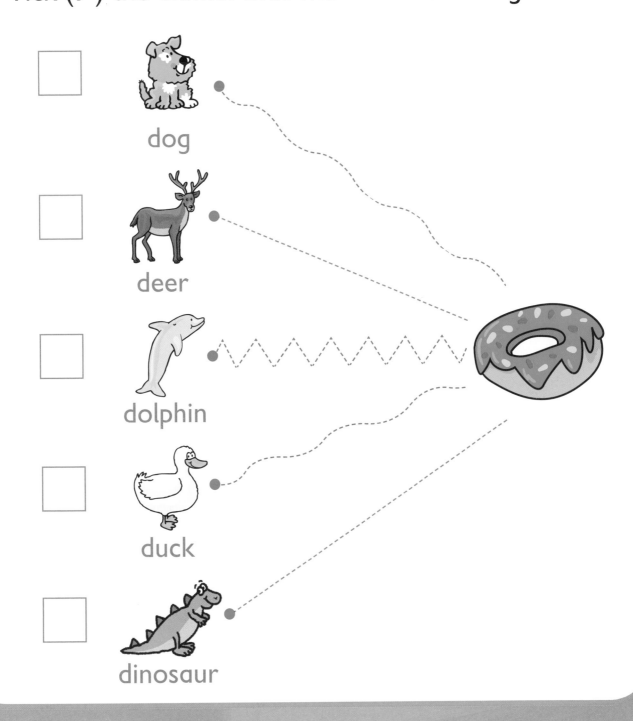

dog

deer

dolphin

duck

dinosaur

Well done!
Now colour
the star.

Phonic sound g

g, as in **gate**.

● Go through the **g**ate and into the **g**arden.
Colour all the things that start with **g**.

A good listening game is sound lotto or sound bingo. If you don't have this game, you can make your own by recording familiar sounds. See if your child can guess what they are or who they are!

Phonic sound o

o, as in **orange**.

● Circle the picture in each row that starts with the **o** sound.

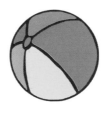   

Well done!
Now colour
the star.

Phonic sound c

c, as in **cat**.

● Colour each picture that starts with the **c** sound.

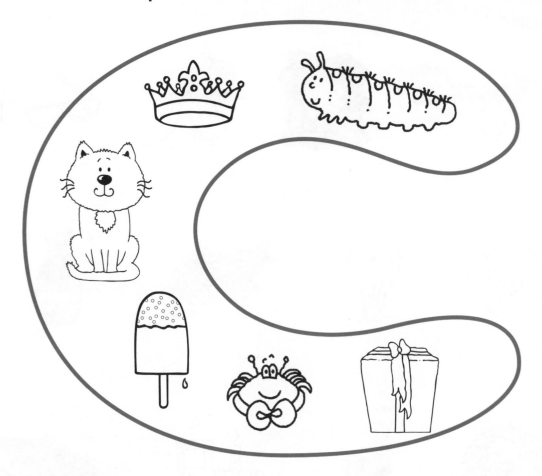

● Write the letter **c** in these words that start the **c** sound.

crayon

clown

cloud

The graphemes **c**, **k**, and **ck** all make the same sound – they are called a 'sound family'. Discuss other **k** sounding words – kite, kangaroo, kettle or names that start with this sound, e.g. Karen, Kellyn, Keith, Kyri.

Phonic sound k and ck

k, as in **kite** and **ck**, as in **clock**.

● Draw a line from each coloured **k**ey to the matching **k**eyhole. Say the **k** sound.

● Circle the **ck** sound in each word.

sock   clock   duck   rocket

Well done!
Now colour
the star.

Phonic sound e

e, as in **egg**.

● Underline the four pictures that start with the **e** sound.

● Trace and copy the letter **e**.

Play a sound matching game. Start with six empty plastic cups and put things inside them to make a sound. Make two of each, for example two with dried rice, two with dried pasta and two with lentils. Cover the tops and then you are ready to play. Shake each cup in turn and try to match the pairs together. If this is too easy, make the sounds more similar by using different amounts of rice, but still two of each.

Phonic sound u

u, as in **umbrella**.

● **Up**, **under** and **umbrella** all start with the **u** sound. Colour the **u** pictures.

● Practise saying the **u** sound when you walk up stairs. Say **u** each time you take a step up: **u u u** …

Well done! Now colour the star.

Phonic sound r

r, as in **red**.

● Circle the picture in each row that starts with the **r** sound.

Play 'I spy'. This game is great to learn and practise initial sounds. Don't forget to make sure the words are phonetic. For example, **unicorn** makes the wrong **u** sound and **ice cream** makes the wrong **i** sound – they do not follow the phonetic rule.

Phonic sound h

h, as in **hat**.

● Draw a **h**at on each **h**orse.

Well done!
Now colour
the star.

Phonic sound b

b, as in **ball**.

● The small pictures show 10 things that start with the **b** sound. Look for these things in the big picture. Tick (✓) each one that you find.

The graphemes **f** and **ff** make the same sound. On the next page, read the **ff** words to your child and help them to hear the **ff** sound. Other **ff** words to discuss could be: puff, cliff, sniff, office, sheriff, cuff, off, takeoff or liftoff.

Phonic sound f and ff

f, as in **fish** and **ff**, as in **puff**.

● Colour each section with a picture that starts with the **f** sound.

● Each of the pictures below has the **ff** sound. Join the dots to finish the word.

coffee

muffin

puffin

Well done!
Now colour
the star.

Phonic sound l and ll

l, as in **ladder** and **ll**, as in **lolly**.

- Join the dots next to the **l** words to make a picture.
  Say each word starting with **l**.

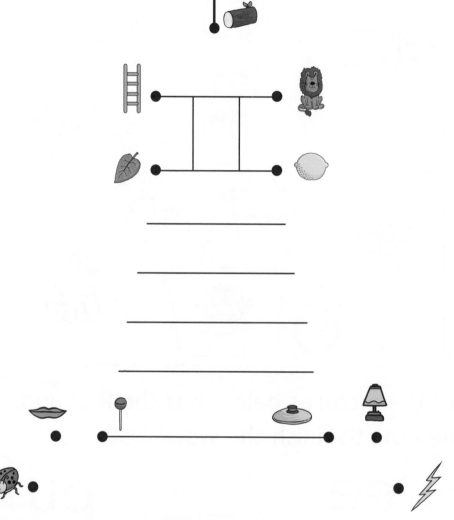

- Say the name for each picture.
  Can you hear the **ll** sound?

Phonic sounds ss and j

ss, as in **dress** and **j**, as in **jelly**.

● Finish these **ss** sounding words.

dress

glass

grass

cross

● Circle each picture that starts with the **j** sound.

Phonic sounds v and w

v, as in **vase** and **w**, as in **water**.

● Draw patterns on the **v**ase, **v**an and **v**est. Practise saying the **v** sound.

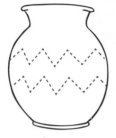  

● Shade each brick with a picture that starts with the **w** sound.

Phonic sounds x and y

x, as in **fox** and **y**, as in **yo-yo**.

● Circle the picture with the **x** sound to show what is in the bo**x**.

● Find the egg **y**olk and **yo-y**o.
Colour them in **y**ellow.

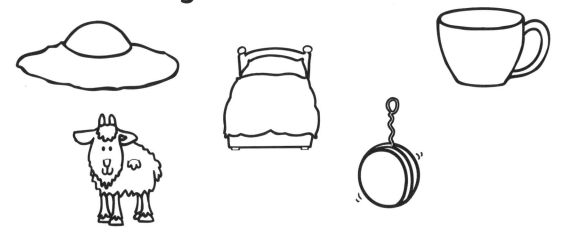

Well done!
Now colour
the star.

Phonic sound z and zz

z, as in **zoo** and **zz**, as in **buzz**.

● Cross out (✗) the picture that does **not** start with the **z** sound.

● Trace the **zz** sound in these words.

pizza

puzzle

buzz

fizzy

Phonic sounds qu and ch

qu, as in **queen** and **ch**, as in **chair**.

● Colour the **qu**een, **qu**ail, **qu**arter and **qu**estion mark.

queen

quail

quarter

question mark

● Circle the pictures that have **ch** at the start.

Phonic sounds sh and th

sh, as in **sheep**, **th**, as in **that** and **th**, as in **thick**.

● Draw a line from each **sh** to the word that begins with that sound.

● Colour the **th** sound in each word below.
Say the **th** sound.
Listen to the different sounds.

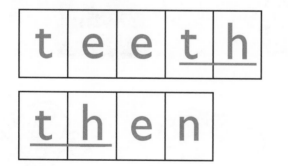

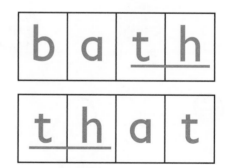

Phonic sounds ng and ai

ng, as in **ring** and **ai**, as in **train**.

● Write **ng** to complete these words.
Say the word and practice the **ng** sound.

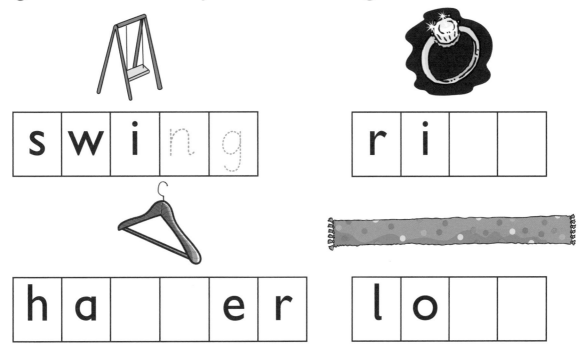

| s | w | i | n | g |

| r | i | | |

| h | a | | e | r |

| l | o | | |

● Say the **ai** sound, as in **tr<u>ai</u>n**.
Match each word to the correct picture using the sounds you have learned.

tr<u>ai</u>n

sn<u>ai</u>l

t<u>ai</u>l

ch<u>ai</u>n

Phonic sound ee

ee, as in **bee**.

● Say each word.
  Tick (✓) the box if you can hear the **ee** sound.

● Circle the **ee** sound in each word.
  Say the **ee** sound.

cheese

teeth

queen

sweet

To read some of these words, you also have to re-visit the **ch**, **th** and **qu** sounds previously learned. These sounds have been underlined, so they represent one sound.

Phonic sound igh

igh, as in **light**.

Can you spot a pattern in these words?
Use the key to colour each letter.

i   g   h

| r | i | g | h | t |

| n | i | g | h | t |

| s | i | g | h | t |

| l | i | g | h | t |

| f | i | g | h | t |

| m | i | g | h | t |

Well done!
Now colour
the star.

Phonic sound oa

oa, as in **boat**.

● Write the **oa** sound in each of the words.
Read the words using the sounds you know.

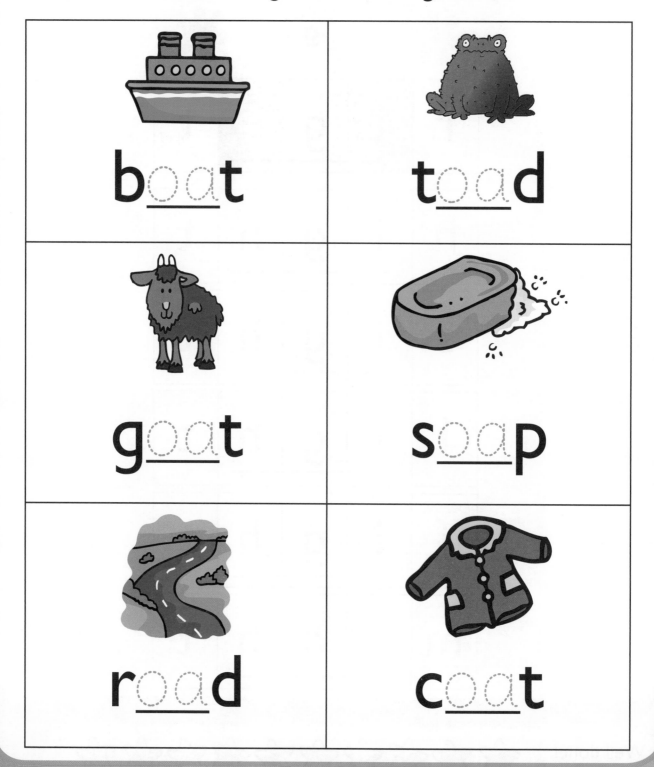

b<u>oa</u>t

t<u>oa</u>d

g<u>oa</u>t

s<u>oa</u>p

r<u>oa</u>d

c<u>oa</u>t

Teach the **oa** sound to your child and then try to read these words together. Say, 'boat, b-oa-t, toad, t-oa-d.'
By splitting the letter sounds up like this, your child will learn that the **oa** is read as a single sound in the word.

Phonic sounds oo

oo, as in **book** and **oo**, as in **moon**.

● Say the **oo** sound heard in **moon**, **spoon** and **broom**.
Then say the **oo** sound heard in **book**, **hook** and **wool**.
Draw a line to match each picture to the correct word.

hook

moon

broom

book

wool

spoon

Phonic sound ar

ar, as in **car**.

- Draw a line to match each picture to the correct word.

st<u>ar</u>   sun

c<u>ar</u>   cat

shoe   sh<u>ar</u>k

<u>ar</u>m   ant

ball   b<u>ar</u>n

p<u>ar</u>k   pip

As with other sounds, the **ar** sound will need to be taught. After completing this book, re-visit all the sounds often. Look at the words and pictures together, so your child will always know and remember which two or three letters, when together, make one sound.

Phonic sounds or and ur

or, as in **fork** and **ur**, as in **nurse**.

● Say the **or** sound.
Circle the picture that matches the word.

fork

horn

cork

corn

● Say the **ur** sound.
Colour each picture and read the word.

nurse

turtle

church

Well done!
Now colour
the star.

Phonic sound ow

ow, as in owl.

● Colour the **ow**l br**ow**n.
  Circle the **ow** sound in the words.

brown owl

● Now colour the pictures and circle the **ow** sound in these words.

clown

crown

cow

More **ow** words that you can discuss include now, down, how, town and towel.

Phonic sound oi

oi, as in **coin**.

- Say the beginning sounds you know and add the **oi** sound.
Draw a line to match each word to the correct picture.

coins

toilet

soil

point

oil

Phonic sound ear

ear, as in **ear**.

- Can you spot a pattern in these words?
  Colour each letter following the key below.

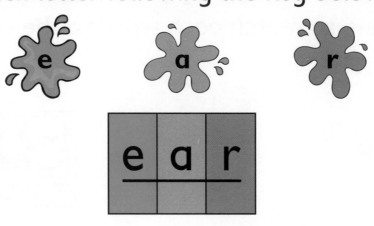

d e a r

n e a r

f e a r

b e a r d

h e a r

y e a r

g e a r

r e a r

These sounds are advanced and your child may need help and encouragement. Don't forget to give lots of praise.

Phonic sound air

air, as in hair.

● Colour the **p**air with **f**air h**air** pointing in the **air**.
Say and circle the **air** sound in each word.

pair fair hair air

Well done!
Now colour
the star.

39

Phonic sound ure

ure, as in **picture**.

● Write **ure** to finish these words.
Say the **ure** sound.

treas u r e

pict___

mixt___

meas___

vult___

Look up or think of more **ure** and **er** words, e.g. sure, cure, assure, insure, mature, secure, rocker, supper, boxer, better. These words are harder to illustrate but can offer lots of discussion. Extending vocabulary and understanding of new words is great to aid future skills in English.

Phonic sound er

er, as in **hammer**.

● Circle each word that has the **er** sound at the end.

banner

Which sound?

● Say the word for each picture.
Choose the correct sound to finish the word and write the letters.

ear   air

f_ _ _

oi   ow

c_ _ _n

ur   ar

c_ _ l

oo   oa

b_ _ t

ch   th

_ _ ick

sh   ff

_ _ eep

Encourage your child to name the picture and then say the two sounds aloud to help identify which is correct.

Answers

Page 4

Accept a circle around 'sundae' also.

Page 5

Page 6

Any colours can be used.

Page 7

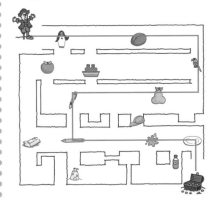

Page 8

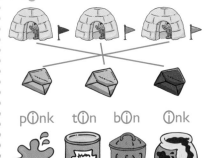

p(i)nk   t(i)n   b(i)n   (i)nk

Page 9

Any colours can be used.

Page 10

(m)elon   (m)ilk   (m)eerkat

(m)oney   (m)onkey

Page 11

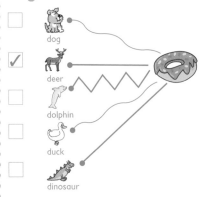

dog
deer ✓
dolphin
duck
dinosaur

Page 12

Any colours can be used.

Page 13

Answers

Page 14

Any colours can be used.

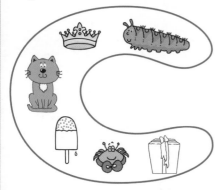

crayon

cloud

clown

Page 15

so(ck) clo(ck) du(ck) ro(ck)et

Page 16

Page 17

Any colours can be used.

Page 18

Page 19

Page 20

Any butterfly can be circled.

Page 21

Any colours can be used.

coffee

muffin

puffin

Page 22

Answers

Page 23

dress

glass

grass

cross

Page 24

Any patterns can be drawn.

Any colour can be used.

Page 25

Page 26

pizza   puzzle

buzz   fizzy

Page 27

Any colours can be used.

queen   quail

quarter   question mark

Page 28

Any colours can be used.

t	e	e	t	h

b	a	t	h

t	h	e	n

t	h	a	t

Page 29

s	w	i	n	g

r	i	n	g

h	a	n	g	e	r

l	o	n	g

train
snail
tail
chain

Page 30

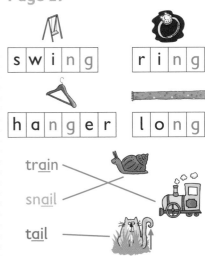

cheese

teeth

queen

sweet

45

Answers

Page 31

| r | i | g | h | t |

| n | i | g | h | t |

| s | i | g | h | t |

| l | i | g | h | t |

| f | i | g | h | t |

| m | i | g | h | t |

Page 32

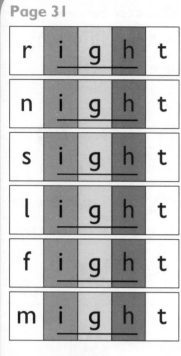

boat — toad

goat — soap

road — coat

Page 33

hook — moon

broom — book — wool

spoon

Page 34

st<u>ar</u> sun   c<u>ar</u> cat

shoe sh<u>ar</u>k   <u>ar</u>m ant

ball b<u>ar</u>n   p<u>ar</u>k pip

Page 35

fork   horn

cork   corn

Any colours can be used.

n<u>ur</u>se   t<u>ur</u>tle   ch<u>ur</u>ch

Page 36

br<u>ow</u>n <u>ow</u>l

Any colours can be used.

clown   cow   crown

Page 37

coins

toilet

soil

point

oil

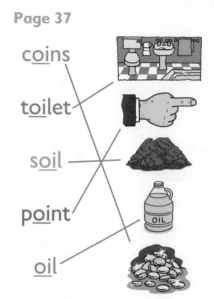

Page 38

d	e a r
f	e a r
h	e a r
g	e a r

n	e a r
b	e a r	d
y	e a r
r	e a r

Page 39

Any colours can be used.

p<u>air</u> f<u>air</u> h<u>air</u> <u>air</u>

Daisy   Maisy

Answers

Page 40

treas**ure**

pict**ure**

mixt**ure**

meas**ure**

vult**ure**

Page 41

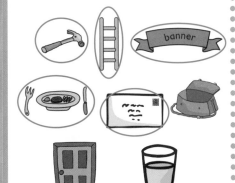

Page 42

fair coin

curl boat

chick sheep

Collins Easy Learning

Certificate of Achievement

Well Done!

This certificate is awarded to ....

for successfully completing ....

Age ....

Date ....

Signed ....

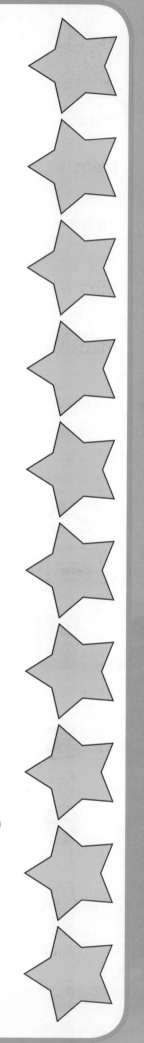